The Wolf's Chicken Stew

Keiko Kasza

 HOUGHTON MIFFLIN

Boston • Atlanta • Dallas • Geneva, Illinois • Palo Alto • Princeton

Houghton Mifflin Edition

Printed in China

ISBN-13: 978-0-395-78153-1
ISBN-10: 0-395-78153-1

ISBN-13: 978-0-618-93271-9
ISBN-10: 0-618-93271-2

1 2 3 4 5 6 7 8 9 SDP 15 14 13 12 11 10 09 08

To Gregory

There once lived a wolf who loved to eat more than anything else in the world. As soon as he finished one meal, he began to think of the next.

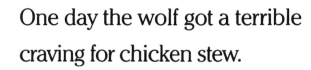

One day the wolf got a terrible craving for chicken stew.

All day long he walked across the forest in search of a delicious chicken. Finally he spotted one.

"Ah, she is just perfect for my stew," he thought.

The wolf crept closer. But just as he was about to grab his prey…

he had another idea.

"If there were just some way to fatten this bird a little more," he thought, "there would be all the more stew for me." So …

the wolf ran home to his kitchen,
and he began to cook.

First he made a hundred scrumptious
pancakes. Then, late at night,
he left them on the chicken's porch.

"Eat well, my pretty chicken,"
he cried. "Get nice and fat for my
stew!"

The next night he brought a
hundred scrumptious doughnuts.
"Eat well, my pretty chicken,"
he cried. "Get nice and fat for my
stew!"

And on the next night he brought
a scrumptious cake weighing a
hundred pounds.

"Eat well, my pretty chicken,"
he cried. "Get nice and fat for my
stew!"

At last, all was ready. This was the night he had been waiting for. He put a large stew pot on the fire and set out joyfully to find his dinner.

"That chicken must be as fat as a
balloon by now," he thought.
"Let's see."

But as he peeked into the
chicken's house...

the door opened suddenly and the chicken screeched, "Oh, so it was you, Mr. Wolf!"

"Children, children! Look, the pancakes and the doughnuts and that scrumptious cake — they weren't from Santa Claus! All those presents were from Uncle Wolf!"

The baby chicks jumped all over
the wolf and gave him a hundred
kisses.

"Oh, thank you, Uncle Wolf!
You're the best cook in the world!"

Uncle Wolf didn't have chicken
stew that night but Mrs. Chicken
fixed him a nice dinner anyway.

"Aw, shucks," he thought, as
he walked home, "maybe tomor-
row I'll bake the little critters a
hundred scrumptious cookies!"